# All Things Bright and Beautiful

© 2012 by Barbour Publishing, Inc.

Written and compiled by Emily Biggers.

Print ISBN 978-1-61626-827-5

eBook Editions:
Adobe Digital Edition (.epub) 978-1-62029-060-6
Kindle and MobiPocket Edition (.prc) 978-1-62029-061-3

Cover and interior design by Koechel Peterson and Associates, Minneapolis, Minnesota.

Published by Barbour Publishing, Inc., P.O. Box 719, Uhrichsville, Ohio 44683, www.barbourbooks.com

*Our mission is to publish and distribute inspirational products offering exceptional value and biblical encouragement to the masses.*

Printed in the United States of America.

# All Things Bright and Beautiful

*inspiration from the beloved hymn*

BARBOUR
PUBLISHING

# Contents

# All Things Bright and Beautiful

*Chorus:*
All things bright and beautiful,
All creatures great and small,
All things wise and wonderful:
The Lord God made them all.

Each little flower that opens,
Each little bird that sings,
He made their glowing colors,
He made their tiny wings.

The purple headed mountains,
The river running by,
The sunset and the morning
That brightens up the sky.

The cold wind in the winter,
The pleasant summer sun,
The ripe fruits in the garden,
He made them every one.

The tall trees in the greenwood,
The meadows where we play,
The rushes by the water,
To gather every day.

He gave us eyes to see them,
And lips that we might tell
How great is God Almighty,
Who has made all things well.

MRS. CECIL F. ALEXANDER, 1848

# Creator and Artist God

Then God said, "Let us make mankind in
our image, in our likeness, so that they may rule
over the fish in the sea and the birds in the sky,
over the livestock and all the wild animals, and over
all the creatures that move along the ground."

GENESIS 1:26 NIV

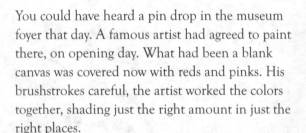

You could have heard a pin drop in the museum
foyer that day. A famous artist had agreed to paint
there, on opening day. What had been a blank
canvas was covered now with reds and pinks. His
brushstrokes careful, the artist worked the colors
together, shading just the right amount in just the
right places.

Before leaving the museum that day, he
declared the painting dedicated to the city, to art
lovers young and old. He snatched up a narrow
tipped brush and added his signature. An original!

We serve an artist God, you know? He looked upon a blank canvas waiting to be filled. He took up His pallet of blues and greens, zebra stripes, and blinding light. He spoke into existence a world of sights and sounds more perfect than any other artist ever dreamed of painting. He brought to life tall giraffes, screeching monkeys, and furry puppies. He crafted collages of pastels around the sun to start and close each day.

But. . .when He had created all of this, the world was not finished. On the sixth day, God made man. You are the signature of Creator God. Made in His image, you bear His name.

To the LORD your God belong the heavens,
even the highest heavens, the earth and everything in it.
Yet the LORD set his affection on your ancestors and
loved them, and he chose you, their descendants,
above all the nations—as it is today.

DEUTERONOMY 10:14–15 NIV

"How great is God—beyond our understanding!
The number of his years is past finding out."

JOB 36:26 NIV

Nature is the art of God.

Thomas Browne

❀

Sunsets are so beautiful that they
almost seem as if we were looking
into the gates of heaven.

John Lubbock

❀

God writes the gospel not in the
Bible alone, but on trees and
flowers and clouds and stars.

Martin Luther

❀

Some people say a man's best
friend is the dog. Mine is nature.

Ward Elliot

*Let the rivers clap their hands,*
*let the mountains sing together for joy.*
PSALM 98:8 NIV

*Now to Him who is able to keep you from stumbling,*
*and to make you stand in the presence of His glory*
*blameless with great joy, to the only God our Savior,*
*through Jesus Christ our Lord, be glory, majesty,*
*dominion and authority, before all time*
*and now and forever. Amen.*
JUDE 1:24–25 NASB

Heavenly Father, so many times
I walk right past the trees. I don't
notice the fluffy white clouds or
appreciate the rain that nurtures
our earth. Your creation is full of
beauty and wonder. I thank You
for this wonderful world that You
have made. May I be more mindful
of Your creation today. Amen.

By faith we understand that the worlds
were framed by the word of God, so that the
things which are seen were not made of
things which are visible.

HEBREWS 11:3 NKJV

❀

The LORD looks down from
heaven on all mankind
to see if there are any who understand,
any who seek God.

PSALM 14:2 NIV

❀

"I have loved you with an everlasting love;
I have drawn you with unfailing kindness."

JEREMIAH 31:3 NIV

After a day of cloud and wind and rain Sometimes the setting sun breaks out again, And touching all the darksome woods with light, Smiles on the fields until they laugh and sing, Then like a ruby from the horizon's ring, Drops down into the night.

HENRY WADSWORTH LONGFELLOW

Rainbows apologize for angry skies.

SYLVIA VOIROL

Who made these beautiful
changing things,
If not one who is beautiful
and changeth not?

SAINT AUGUSTINE

*I look to the hills!*
*Where will I find help?*
*It will come from the LORD,*
*who created the heavens*
*and the earth.*

PSALM 121:1–2 CEV

*Then God blessed the seventh day*
*and made it holy, because on it he rested from*
*all the work of creating that he had done.*

<small>GENESIS 2:3 NIV</small>

Father, I pray that You will reveal Yourself to me through creation today. Open my eyes that I might see You in the beauty of the world around me. Open my ears that I might hear You in nature. Clear my mind of everything else. Set my thoughts on You and on Your ways. Walk with me. Talk with me. I ask these things in the name of Your Son, Jesus. Amen.

God, that all-powerful Creator of
nature and architect of the world,
has impressed man with no character
so proper to distinguish him from other
animals, as by the faculty of speech.

QUINTILIAN

❧

God of the forests and trees!
Color our lives with love and compassion.
Source of all beauty and truth!
Help us to live as shade for the weary
Hope for the broken and
home for the lost.

MARTY HAUGEN

# The Heavens Declare the Glory of the Lord

*he heavens declare the glory of God;
the skies proclaim the work of his hands.*

PSALM 19:1 NIV

❧

Jenn had prepared for this night for months. Her voice coach suggested resting on the day of the performance, but she had sneaked in a rehearsal that afternoon. She wanted the song to be perfect.

The church was packed. Jenn's song was beautiful. The praise band didn't miss a beat, and the lighting added so much to the presentation. While Jenn knew that the praise should go to God, she couldn't help feeling a bit of pride as the congregation stood and clapped when she had finished that last high note.

Driving home that night down a country road, Jenn noticed the stars shining brightly against the backdrop of the black sky. At the sight of the vast array of twinkling lights, Jenn wept. Away from the crowded church, in the stillness of God's creation, she realized that her song had been for her own glory.

The next time Jenn sang in church, her heart had changed. She didn't worry about her appearance or the perfection of the notes. She used her musical gifts to bring glory to the Father—just as the stars in the night sky do.

The heavens declare the glory of the Lord. Likewise, may we.

*For the LORD is great and greatly to be praised;*
*He is also to be feared above all gods.*
*For all the gods of the peoples are idols,*
*But the LORD made the heavens.*
*Honor and majesty are before Him;*
*Strength and gladness are in His place.*

1 CHRONICLES 16: 25–27 NKJV

❀

*For you make me glad by your deeds, LORD;*
*I sing for joy at what your hands have done.*

PSALM 92:4 NIV

Summer and winter,
and springtime and harvest,
Sun, moon, and stars
in their courses above,
Join with all nature
in manifold witness
To Thy great faithfulness,
mercy and love.

FROM "GREAT IS THY FAITHFULNESS"
THOMAS OBADIAH CHISOLM

Aim at heaven and you will
get earth thrown in. Aim at
earth and you get neither.

C. S. LEWIS

My home is in heaven.
I'm just traveling through this world.

BILLY GRAHAM

*The Son is the radiance of God's glory and the exact
representation of his being, sustaining all things by his
powerful word. After he had provided purification for sins,
he sat down at the right hand of the Majesty in heaven.*

HEBREWS 1:3 NIV

*God looks down from heaven on all mankind to see if
there are any who understand, any who seek God.*

PSALM 53:2 NIV

Sovereign God, I praise Your holy name. You were before all things. You made all things. And You desire that Your creation praise You. Regardless of my circumstances, I will praise You, Lord! I will tell of our work in my life. I will testify that You are the one true God. I will always give You praise. Amen.

Let them praise the name of the LORD,
For His name alone is exalted;
His glory is above the earth and heaven.
And He has exalted the horn of His people,
The praise of all His saints—
Of the children of Israel,
A people near to Him.
Praise the LORD!

PSALM 148:13-14 NKJV

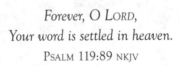

Forever, O LORD,
Your word is settled in heaven.

PSALM 119:89 NKJV

The sky is the daily
bread of the eyes.
RALPH WALDO EMERSON

Fair is the sunshine,
fairer still the moonlight,
And all the twinkling starry host;
Jesus shines brighter, Jesus shines purer
Than all the angels heaven can boast.
FROM "FAIREST LORD JESUS"

To see the summer sky is poetry,
though never in a book it lie—
true poems flee.
EMILY DICKINSON

*Listen, you heavens, and I will speak;*
*hear, you earth, the words of my mouth.*
*Let my teaching fall like rain*
*and my words descend like dew,*
*like showers on new grass,*
*like abundant rain on tender plants.*
*I will proclaim the name of the L*ORD*.*
*Oh, praise the greatness of our God!*

God, I am amazed to think that I was made in Your image! Your very finger-prints are on my form. You thought of me before my parents did. You hid me in the secret safety of my mother's womb. I am fearfully and wonderfully made. May I live to glorify my Creator! May I join with all creation to sing glory to God! Amen.

Well, let me remind you it all matters
as long as you do everything you do to
the glory of the One who made you!

STEVEN CURTIS CHAPMAN

❖

A teardrop on earth summons
the King of heaven.

CHARLES R. SWINDOLL

❖

God is the Creator; Satan is the counterfeiter.

EDWIN LOUIS COLE

❖

The universe is centered on neither the
earth nor the sun. It is centered on God.

ALFRED NOYES

# A Peace That Passes Understanding

*Be anxious for nothing, but in everything by prayer and supplication, with thanksgiving, let your requests be made known to God; and the peace of God, which surpasses all understanding, will guard your hearts and minds through Christ Jesus.*

PHILIPPIANS 4:6–7 NKJV

Have you ever been tempted to purchase a cheap imitation of the real thing?

Remember that purse the sidewalk vendor tried to pass off as a designer one? You knew it wasn't real (no way, at that low price!) but you wondered if others would notice the subtle differences. It sure *looked* authentic.

Ever buy an off-brand appliance only to call a repairman the next month? You have to admit the old saying is usually true—"You get what you pay for!"

God wants to bless you with peace that is superior to what the world offers. The world declares loudly through billboards and television that material things will bring you peace. Satan may tempt you with a relationship or choice that you know is not God's best. In the end, these empty promises will leave you anything but peaceful.

God made you. He knows you from the inside out. He knows what will fill the empty spots in your heart and calm the storms that overwhelm you. Your Creator does not offer a cheap imitation. He is the real deal. Seek Him, and you will experience a peace that cannot be contained in words, a peace that passes understanding.

"These things I have spoken to you, so that in Me you
may have peace. In the world you have tribulation,
but take courage; I have overcome the world."

JOHN 16:33 NASB

He will make your righteous reward shine like the dawn,
your vindication like the noonday sun.

PSALM 37:6 NIV

Peace on the outside comes from
knowing God on the inside.

UNKNOWN

When you are proclaiming peace
with your lips, be careful to have
it even more fully in your heart.

ST. FRANCIS OF ASSISI

I believe that God is in me as the
sun is in the color and fragrance of a
flower—the light in my darkness,
the voice in my silence.

HELEN KELLER

*Those who hope in the LORD will renew their strength.*
*They will soar on wings like eagles; they will run and not*
*grow weary, they will walk and not be faint.*
ISAIAH 40:31 NIV

*The name of the LORD is a fortified tower;*
*the righteous run to it and are safe.*
PROVERBS 18:10 NIV

Heavenly Father, help me today to seek the peace that passes all human understanding. Remind me that true peace can only be found when I am walking with You. When I look to my left or to my right, set my feet straight upon the path again. I want to walk in Your ways. I desire Your peace in my life. Amen.

"And the LORD will continually guide you, and satisfy your desire in scorched places, and give strength to your bones; and you will be like a watered garden, and like a spring of water whose waters do not fail."

ISAIAH 58:11 NASB

Again Jesus said, "Peace be with you! As the Father has sent me, I am sending you." And with that he breathed on them and said, "Receive the Holy Spirit."

JOHN 20:21–23 NIV

Although the world is full of suffering,
it is full also of the overcoming of it.

HELEN KELLER

God cannot give us a happiness and
peace apart from Himself, because it is
not there. There is no such thing.

C. S. LEWIS

If we had no winter, the spring would
not be so pleasant: if we did not sometimes taste of adversity, prosperity
would not be so welcome.

ANNE BRADSTREET

*Therefore, since we have been justified through faith,*
*we have peace with God through our Lord Jesus Christ,*
*through whom we have gained access by faith into*
*this grace in which we now stand. And we boast*
*in the hope of the glory of God.*

ROMANS 5:1–2 NIV

*The LORD is near to the brokenhearted*
*and saves those who are crushed in spirit.*

PSALM 34:18 NASB

Lord, Your Word tells me to be anxious for nothing. I find myself anxious at times. I worry. I try to run up ahead of You rather than letting You lead the way. Calm my spirit, Lord, as only You can do. Help me to find You in the stillness of this moment. In Jesus' name I pray, amen.

It is not so much for its beauty that the forest
makes a claim upon men's hearts, as for that
subtle something, that quality of air, that
emanation from old trees, that so wonderfully
changes and renews a weary spirit.

ROBERT LOUIS STEVENSON

Happiness does not come from without,
it comes from within.

HELEN KELLER

Peace is not the absence of affliction,
but the presence of God.

UNKNOWN

# All Creatures Great and Small

*But God chose the foolish things of this world to put the wise to shame. He chose the weak things of this world to put the powerful to shame.*
1 CORINTHIANS 1:27 CEV

❧

God's economy is different from any other. The world places a high value on material wealth, physical strength, and outward beauty. Throughout God's Word, He makes it clear that this is not what He looks for in His creation. God looks at the heart.

Perhaps in your family or among your coworkers, you feel small or unnoticed. Have you been passed over for a promotion? Are you unsure your contributions matter, perhaps a bit envious of those who seem to always outdo your best efforts?

The Bible is full of examples of "small" people who made a big impact. Zaccheus was small in stature but, upon meeting Christ, showed great character when he repaid those from whom he had stolen. Jesus even went home with Zaccheus! David was but a young shepherd boy when God chose him to slay the giant Goliath. God used a prostitute, a young boy with a sack lunch, and even a former murderer of Christians to do great things for the kingdom.

The next time you feel as if you are not making much of a difference at all, remember that your Creator uses the small to do great things. God sees your great value.

*Then the LORD God took the man and put him into the
garden of Eden to cultivate it and keep it.*

GENESIS 2:15 NASB

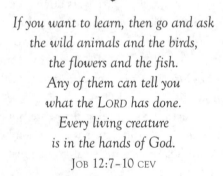

*If you want to learn, then go and ask
the wild animals and the birds,
the flowers and the fish.
Any of them can tell you
what the LORD has done.
Every living creature
is in the hands of God.*

JOB 12:7-10 CEV

You must not know too much, or be too
precise or scientific about birds and trees
and flowers and watercraft; a certain free
margin, and even vagueness. . .helps
your enjoyment of these things.

WALT WHITMAN

Have you ever observed a hummingbird
moving about in an aerial dance among
the flowers—a living prismatic gem. . . .
It is a creature of such fairy-like
loveliness as to mock all description.

W. H. HUDSON

"Look at the birds of the air; they do not sow or reap or store away in barns, and yet your heavenly Father feeds them. Are you not much more valuable than they?"

MATTHEW 6:26 NIV

The wolf will live with the lamb,
the leopard will lie down with the goat,
the calf and the lion and the yearling together;
and a little child will lead them.

ISAIAH 11:6 NIV

Life gets so busy, God. Too busy.
Let me take time to smell the roses
today! You have created a world full
of flowers and trees, amazing creatures such as the squirrels that dart
across my yard and the birds whose
songs provide a free concert if only I
will slow down long enough to listen!
Help me to slow down today. Amen.

*As each one has received a gift, minister it to one
another, as good stewards of the manifold grace of God.
. . . If anyone ministers, let him do it as with the ability
which God supplies, that in all things God may
be glorified through Jesus Christ.*

1 Peter 4:10–11 nkjv

*The righteous care for the needs of their animals,
but the kindest acts of the wicked are cruel.*

Proverbs 12:10 niv

If you have men who will exclude any of God's creatures from the shelter of compassion and pity, you will have men who will deal likewise with their fellow men.

ST. FRANCIS OF ASSISI

You don't have a soul. You are a Soul. You have a body.

C. S. LEWIS

God's gifts put man's best dreams to shame.

ELIZABETH BARRETT BROWNING

And every creature which is in heaven and on the earth
and under the earth and such as are in the sea,
and all that are in them, I heard saying:
"Blessing and honor and glory and power
be to Him who sits on the throne,
and to the Lamb, forever and ever!"

REVELATION 5:13 NKJV

It is in the quiet that I find You, Father.
Help me not to be afraid to be still.
Whether in the warmth of sunshine
or listening to the soft rain fall, speak
to me. I am listening. I want to meet
with You today. I long to find the quiet
strength I often forfeit as I lose myself
in the noise of the world. Amen.

I am careful not to confuse excellence
with perfection. Excellence, I can reach for;
perfection is God's business.

MICHAEL J. FOX

No one can make you feel
inferior without your consent.

ELEANOR ROOSEVELT

Self-pity is our worst enemy and
if we yield to it, we can never
do anything wise in the world.

HELEN KELLER

If you put a small value on yourself,
rest assured that the world will
not raise your price.

UNKNOWN

# God's Amazing Imagination

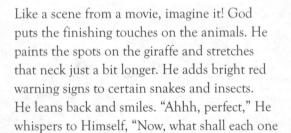

*Now the LORD God had formed out of the ground all the wild animals and all the birds in the sky. He brought them to the man to see what he would name them; and whatever the man called each living creature, that was its name. So the man gave names to all the livestock, the birds in the sky and all the wild animals.*

GENESIS 2:19–20 NIV

Like a scene from a movie, imagine it! God puts the finishing touches on the animals. He paints the spots on the giraffe and stretches that neck just a bit longer. He adds bright red warning signs to certain snakes and insects. He leans back and smiles. "Ahhh, perfect," He whispers to Himself, "Now, what shall each one be called?"

Oh, God could have named them Himself. His creativity speaks for itself in the zebra's bold stripes and the howling of jungle monkeys! No help was necessary in deciding upon their names. But like the parent who allows a child to stir the cake batter or help paint the garage, God gave this job to Adam.

Imagine it! A parade of animals in the Garden of Eden, each one uniquely crafted by its Creator, passes by Adam. How long the first man must have pondered some of those names—"butterfly," "hippopotamus," "boa constrictor," "camel."

All it takes is a look around His world to know that God has an amazing imagination! Each tree and flower, each animal and insect bears intricate symmetry and beauty. One can almost see the fingerprints of God upon His creation!

*The L*ORD *God said, "It isn't good for the man to live
alone. I need to make a suitable partner for him."*
GENESIS 2:18 CEV

*All Your works shall praise You, O L*ORD,
*and Your saints shall bless You.*
PSALM 145:10 NKJV

*"You, L*ORD, *in the beginning
laid the foundation of the earth,
And the heavens are the work of Your hands."*
HEBREWS 1:10 NKJV

Nature never goes out of style.
UNKNOWN

There is not a sprig of grass that
shoots uninteresting to me.
THOMAS JEFFERSON

Half the interest of a garden is the
constant exercise of the imagination.
MRS. C. W. EARLE

Nature is full of genius, full of the
divinity; so that not a snowflake
escapes its fashioning hand.
HENRY DAVID THOREAU

*Then God said, "Let there be light"; and there was*
*light. And God saw the light, that it was good; and*
*God divided the light from the darkness. God called*
*the light Day, and the darkness He called Night.*
*So the evening and the morning were the first day.*

GENESIS 1:3–5 NKJV

*For He commands and raises the stormy wind,*
*Which lifts up the waves of the sea.*

PSALM 107:25 NKJV

You are an artist extraordinaire, Lord. As I look at the world around me, I see a glimmer of Your creativity. The colors and splendor of Your creation reveal a bit of the artist's mind. One day I will know fully, even as I am fully known by You. Until then, may I never cease to be amazed by Your creation. I see You in it. I marvel at Your goodness. Amen.

For behold, He who forms mountains and creates the wind
And declares to man what are His thoughts,
He who makes dawn into darkness
And treads on the high places of the earth,
The LORD God of hosts is His name.

AMOS 4:13 NASB

"For to the snow He says, 'Fall on the earth,'
And to the downpour and the rain, 'Be strong.'"

JOB 37:6 NASB

Winter is an etching, spring a
watercolor, summer an oil painting,
and autumn a mosaic of them all.

STANLEY HOROWITZ

❖

The tulip and the butterfly
Appear in gayer coats than I:
Let me be dressed fine as I will,
Flies, worms, and flowers exceed me still.

ISAAC WATTS

❖

Beauty is God's handwriting.

CHARLES KINGSLEY

❖

We can learn a lot from trees:
they're always grounded but never
stop reaching heavenward.

EVERETT MAMOR

He cuts out channels in the rocks,
And his eye sees every precious thing.

JOB 28:10 NKJV

When He utters His voice—
There is a multitude of waters in the heavens:
"He causes the vapors to ascend from the ends of the earth;
He makes lightnings for the rain;
He brings the wind out of His treasuries."

JEREMIAH 51:16 NKJV

God, every day it seems there is a new invention! Technology has gotten so creative, God, but it will never measure up to Your imagination. Your hands designed this world and made everything in it. The artwork in the most famous museums does not begin to compare to Your creation! I love You and I praise You. Amen.

*For me, the world of nature bears spectacular witness to the imaginative genius of our Creator.*
PHILLIP YANCEY

*And when it rains on your parade, look up rather than down. Without the rain, there would be no rainbow.*
GILBERT K. CHESTERTON

*Spring is nature's way of saying, "Let's party!"*
ROBIN WILLIAMS

# Fearfully and Wonderfully Made

*od created man in His own image,*
*in the image of God He created him;*
*male and female He created them.*

GENESIS 1:27 NASB

❀

There is nothing like a newborn baby to turn our thoughts toward the Creator. Ten tiny fingers and toes, the first cry, sweet gurgles and coos. . . . As many babies as one has seen, new life never ceases to amaze.

Humanity does not just exist. A big bang did not result in the intricate detail called life. Nor did we evolve from apes. While they are amazing creatures, they are not the creations God called "man" and "woman." The Bible teaches that God made man different. He made us in His image.

Certainly a tiny baby is a reminder of the miracle of life. But when was the last time you looked in the mirror? Do you realize that you are *fearfully and wonderfully made*? It may have been a few years back now, but God thought you up! He designed you. The Bible says He knit you together in your mother's womb (see Psalm 139:13). And He is pleased with His creation.

You are made in the image of the Lord Almighty. He loves you immensely. You are more important to Him than the birds of the air or the fish of the sea. You are His ultimate masterpiece. You are His child.

My frame was not hidden from you
when I was made in the secret place,
when I was woven together in the depths of
the earth. Your eyes saw my unformed body;
all the days ordained for me were written in
your book before one of them came to be.

PSALM 139:15–16 NIV

Charm is deceitful and beauty is vain,
But a woman who fears the LORD, she shall be praised.

PROVERBS 31:30 NASB

God, remind me today that You do not make mistakes. I am not intended to be like everyone else. I am designed to be just the person You created me to be. Help me to use my gifts and abilities to glorify You. Let me honor You in all that I say and do today. Amen.

When I consider Your heavens, the work of Your fingers,
The moon and the stars, which You have ordained,
What is man that You are mindful of him,
And the son of man that You visit him?
For You have made him a little lower than the angels,
And You have crowned him with glory and honor.
PSALM 8:3–5 NKJV

God loves each of us as if
there were only one of us.

AUGUSTINE

I've never seen a smiling
face that was not beautiful.

UNKNOWN

Let the rain kiss you. Let the rain beat
upon your head with silver liquid drops.
Let the rain sing you a lullaby.

LANGSTON HUGHES

*For you created my inmost being; you knit me together in my mother's womb. I praise you because I am fearfully and wonderfully made; your works are wonderful, I know that full well.*

PSALM 139:13–14 NIV

*"For God so loved the world that He gave His only begotten Son, that whoever believes in Him should not perish but have everlasting life."*

JOHN 3:16 NKJV

Father, because I was made in Your image, please help me to reflect Your character to the world. When my friends look at me, I pray that they will see Your faithfulness. When I encounter strangers, may they get a glimpse of Your love even through a smile or a kind word spoken. Use me as a reflection of Your love that the world might come to know You, sovereign God. Amen.

*So the LORD God caused a deep sleep to fall upon the man, and he slept; then He took one of his ribs and closed up the flesh at that place. The LORD God fashioned into a woman the rib which He had taken from the man, and brought her to the man.*

GENESIS 2:21–22 NASB

The things that make me different
are the things that make me.

A. A. MILNE

Is your place a small place?
Tend it with care; He set you there.
Is your place a large place?
Guard it with care! He set you there.
Whate'er your place, it is not yours alone,
but his who set you there.

JOHN OXENHAM

Is your place a small place?

All that God requires of us is an
opportunity to show what He can do.

A. B. SIMPSON

79

*Shout for joy to the L*ORD*, all the earth.*
*Worship the L*ORD *with gladness;*
*come before him with joyful songs.*
*Know that the L*ORD *is God.*
*It is he who made us, and we are his;*
*we are his people, the sheep of his pasture.*

PSALM 100:1–3 NIV

*The Spirit of God has made me,*
*And the breath of the Almighty gives me life.*

JOB 33:4 NKJV

Heavenly Father, some days it is really hard to feel good about myself. I feel a little clumsier and a little less polished than my coworkers and friends. Teach me to see myself through a lens of grace. Teach me to strive to always do my best but also to find rest in being less than perfect. I love You, Lord. Amen.

To fall in love with God is the greatest of all
romances; to seek him, the greatest adventure;
to find him, the greatest human achievement.

RAPHAEL SIMON

What a friend we have in Jesus, all our
sins and griefs to bear. What a privilege
to carry everything to God in prayer.

JOSEPH SCRIVEN

The gateway to Christianity is not through
an intricate labyrinth of dogma, but by a
simple belief in the person of Christ.

NORMAN VINCENT PEALE

He Knows
Our Hearts

*"Indeed, the very hairs of your head
are all numbered. Do not fear; you are
more valuable than many sparrows."*

LUKE 12:7 NASB

Yolanda's classroom was a magical place. Education students from the local college were often sent to observe this phenomenal teacher. The test scores from Yolanda's class were always among the best in the school, and her students read at higher levels than expected for the second grade. But academic achievements aside, there was just something special about the way this educator interacted with her students.

Yolanda knew her students. She knew more than just their names and the grades they had made on the last spelling test. She knew their hobbies, their preferences, little bits of trivia about their families. Yolanda knew the children's hearts.

God knows His children like that. When our Father looks down from heaven, He does not just see a group of human beings. He sees individuals. The Bible says He knows the number of hairs on your head. He knows your desires and dreams, your strengths and weaknesses. Talk to God today. Tell Him what you are worried about. Ask Him for help. He knows your heart, and He longs to spend time with you, His precious daughter.

*For I command you today to love the LORD
your God, to walk in obedience to him, and to keep
his commands, decrees and laws; then you will live
and increase, and the LORD your God will bless
you in the land you are entering to possess.*

DEUTERONOMY 30:16 NIV

*But Jesus often withdrew to lonely places and prayed.*

LUKE 5:16 NIV

I find comfort, Lord, in knowing that You know me. Even in my imperfection, You love me. You created me. I am Yours. You see me as righteous because I have accepted Your Son as my righteousness. You see me as Your daughter, made in Your image. You long to spend time with me. It feels good to be loved by You. Amen.

*The LORD is compassionate and gracious, slow to anger and abounding in lovingkindness. He will not always strive with us, nor will He keep His anger forever.*

PSALM 103:8–9 NASB

*Before a word is on my tongue
you, LORD, know it completely.
You hem me in behind and before,
and you lay your hand upon me.
Such knowledge is too wonderful for me,
too lofty for me to attain.*

PSALM 139:4–6 NIV

God's promises are like the stars;
the darker the night the
brighter they shine.

DAVID NICHOLAS

Lord, considering Your concern for
even the sparrow brings joy to my
soul this day—knowing that You
care infinitely more for me.

LEE WARREN

Those who dwell among the
beauties and mysteries of the earth
are never alone or weary of life.

RACHEL CARSON

*Behold what manner of love the Father has bestowed*
*on us, that we should be called children of God!*
1 John 3:1 NKJV

*So whether you eat or drink or whatever you do,*
*do it all for the glory of God.*
1 Corinthians 10:31 NIV

*You have searched me, Lord,*
*and you know me.*
*You know when I sit and when I rise;*
*you perceive my thoughts from afar.*
Psalm 139:1-2 NIV

In this great big world, God, how is it that You see me? With all the bigger problems, why do You care about mine? It is beyond my comprehension that the Creator of the universe knows my heart and cares to listen to my prayers. Thank You, Lord, for never leaving me alone. Thank You for listening to me. Amen.

"Acknowledge the God of your father, and serve him with wholehearted devotion and with a willing mind, for the LORD searches every heart and understands every desire and every thought. If you seek him, he will be found by you; but if you forsake him, he will reject you forever."

1 CHRONICLES 28:9 NIV

Many are the plans in a person's heart,
but it is the LORD's purpose that prevails.

PROVERBS 19:21 NIV

Keep love in your heart. A life without it is like a sunless garden when the flowers are dead. The consciousness of loving and being loved brings a warmth and richness to life that nothing else can bring.

OSCAR WILDE

Everybody needs beauty as well as bread, places to play in and pray in.

JOHN MUIR

When we put our cares in His hands, He puts His peace in our hearts.

UNKNOWN

*Search me, God, and know my heart;*
*test me and know my anxious thoughts.*
*See if there is any offensive way in me,*
*and lead me in the way everlasting.*
PSALM 139:23–24 NIV

*For now we see only a reflection as in a mirror;*
*then we shall see face to face. Now I know in part;*
*then I shall know fully, even as I am fully known.*
1 CORINTHIANS 13:12 NIV

Father, I think everyone wants to be known. I hear so many people saying, "No one understands me!" In our limited humanity, we can't fully understand another's burden, grief, or fears. I take comfort knowing that You know me fully. You understand my weaknesses, and amazingly, You love me still. Thank You for knowing me and for never giving up on me. In Jesus' name I pray, amen.

The beauty of creation convinces me
that the Creator not only loves me,
but He wants me to have the very best.

UNKNOWN

Let God's promises shine on your problems.

CORRIE TEN BOOM

The more we depend on God the
more dependable we find He is.

CLIFF RICHARD

If God is your partner,
make your plans BIG!

D. L. MOODY

# All Things
# Wise and
# Wonderful

The law of the LORD is perfect,
refreshing the soul. The statutes of the LORD
are trustworthy, making wise the simple.

PSALM 19:7 NIV

❀

Have you been so thirsty that you simply
couldn't wait to get a drink? As a drink of cold
water satisfies a parched mouth, God's Word
refreshes the soul that drinks deep of its truths.
As a believer, you may not always understand
why God's Word instructs you in a certain
manner. In such times, trust that your loving
heavenly Father has only your best interest at
heart.

Wisdom is offered to the Christian who
follows the ways of the Lord. Consider a true
disciple of Jesus, perhaps an older person in
your church fellowship that you would describe

as wise. Undoubtedly, that individual's life story contains decision points between the ways of the world and God's ways.

Choose to drink deep of the law of the Lord. Meditate on His scriptures. When your sin nature pulls you one direction but God's Word directs in another, you will never be disappointed if you choose God. His ways are perfect, and His law is designed to give you abundant life. As you grow in the wisdom of the Lord, you will find wonderful blessing. All things wise and wonderful. . .come from your Father.

My message and my preaching were not with wise
and persuasive words, but with a demonstration of
the Spirit's power, so that your faith might not
rest on human wisdom, but on God's power.

1 CORINTHIANS 2:4–5 NIV

For we know that if the earthly tent we live in is
destroyed, we have a building from God, an eternal
house in heaven, not built by human hands.

2 CORINTHIANS 5:1 NIV

God, I have always admired the great scholars. They even *look* wise! But You are the wisest of all, Lord, and the wisdom from above is different from knowledge one can gain in this world. You are the Alpha and the Omega, the beginning and the end. Your wisdom surpasses that of the wisest scholars. Teach me, Lord. Show me Your ways. Give me godly wisdom for the decisions I must make. Amen.

*He commanded our ancestors to teach their children,
so the next generation would know them, even the
children yet to be born, and they in turn
would tell their children.*

PSALM 78:5-6 NIV

*Do not be wise in your own eyes; fear the LORD
and turn away from evil. It will be healing to
your body and refreshment to your bones.*

PROVERBS 3:7-8 NASB

Earth and sky, woods and fields,
lakes and rivers, the mountain and
the sea, are excellent schoolmasters,
and teach us more than we can
ever learn from books.

JOHN LUBBOCK

Some people, in order to discover God,
read books. But there is a great book: the
very appearance of created things. Look
above you! Look below you! Read it.

AUGUSTINE

I cannot imagine how the
clockwork of the universe can
exist without a clockmaker.

VOLTAIRE

*Now God gave Solomon wisdom and very great discernment and breadth of mind, like the sand that is on the seashore. Solomon's wisdom surpassed the wisdom of all the sons of the east and all the wisdom of Egypt.*

1 KINGS 4:29–30 NASB

*Conduct yourselves with wisdom toward outsiders, making the most of the opportunity.*

COLOSSIANS 4:5 NASB

Lord, in times when I need godly counsel, lead me to those who seek wisdom from above. There are so many voices that compete for my listening ear! Help me, Father, to discern the right from the wrong, those who will lead me closer to You from those who will lead me astray. I ask You for godly wisdom. In Jesus' Name, amen.

For, "All people are like grass, and all their glory is like the flowers of the field; the grass withers and the flowers fall, but the word of the Lord endures forever." And this is the word that was preached to you.

1 PETER 1:24–25 NIV

Give me understanding, and I shall keep Your law; Indeed, I shall observe it with my whole heart.

PSALM 119:34 NKJV

Earth is crammed with heaven
And every bush aflame with God
But only those who see take
off their shoes.

ELIZABETH BARRETT BROWNING

The Bible is the only credible guide
either as to the real relationship
between man and the earth and the great
Creator of both or concerning the
purpose of the creation of both.

JOSEPH FRANKLIN RUTHERFORD

In every walk with nature one
receives far more than he seeks.

JOHN MUIR

For who knows a person's thoughts except their own spirit within them? In the same way no one knows the thoughts of God except the Spirit of God. What we have received is not the spirit of the world, but the Spirit who is from God, so that we may understand what God has freely given us.

1 CORINTHIANS 2:11–12 NIV

# Light of the World

*You are the light of the world. A town built on a hill cannot be hidden. Neither do people light a lamp and put it under a bowl. Instead they put it on its stand, and it gives light to everyone in the house. In the same way, let your light shine before others, that they may see your good deeds and glorify your Father in heaven."*

MATTHEW 5:14-16 NIV

Have you been outside in the country after dark? The stars illuminate the sky. They are big and bold and above all, they are bright! In the city, stars are not nearly as eye-catching.

They are the same stars. It is pollution that clouds their brilliance.

Are you a country star or a city star? It might seem like an odd question at first, but consider it.

Our charge as Christ followers is to be the light of the world!

Bright light.

Illuminating light.

Difference-making light.

Light that causes those around us to desire it for themselves.

Light that shines in the darkness.

Country star kind of light!

Has the world polluted your light? With lives crowded with constant technology and trying to keep up with the latest trends, do we shine as brightly? Do we look different as believers, or do we blend in nicely with the world?

Can others see your light? Is it bright. . .or is it dim? Jesus taught His followers that they were to be the light of the world. As His disciples in the twenty-first century, we are called to be this same light. Ask God to help you shine for Him.

*But the path of the righteous is like the light of dawn,*
*That shines brighter and brighter until the full day.*

PROVERBS 4:18 NASB

❀

*Even in darkness light dawns for the upright, for those*
*who are gracious and compassionate and righteous.*

PSALM 112:4 NIV

❀

*For he chose us in him before the creation of*
*the world to be holy and blameless in his sight.*

EPHESIANS 1:4 NIV

All the darkness of the world cannot
extinguish the light of a small candle.

St. Francis of Assisi

The sun is. . .warmth-giving
and happiness-giving.

Jessi Lane Adams

A single sunbeam is enough
to drive away many shadows.

St. Francis of Assisi

For light I go directly to the source
of light, not to any of the reflections.

Peace Pilgrim

"Light has come into the world, but people loved darkness instead of light because their deeds were evil. Everyone who does evil hates the light, and will not come into the light for fear that their deeds will be exposed. But whoever lives by the truth comes into the light, so that it may be seen plainly that what they have done has been done in the sight of God."

JOHN 3:19-21 NIV

Jesus, light of the world, You are the way, the truth, and the life. You are the Redeemer, my Savior, and amazingly enough. . .You are also my friend. Give me the strength that it takes to shine for You in the darkness of this world. It is easier to dim my light. I long to shine it before others that they might see my good works and glorify my God. Amen.

*The precepts of the L<small>ORD</small> are right, rejoicing the heart;*
*The commandment of the L<small>ORD</small> is pure,*
*enlightening the eyes.*

<small>PSALM</small> 19:8 <small>NASB</small>

*God made two great lights—the greater light to govern*
*the day and the lesser light to govern the night.*
*He also made the stars.*

<small>GENESIS</small> 1:16 <small>NIV</small>

Where there is sunshine
the doctor starves.

FLEMISH PROVERB

Lord, make me an instrument
of thy peace.
Where there is hatred, let me sow love,
Where there is injury, pardon;
Where there is doubt, faith;
Where there is despair, hope;
Where there is darkness, light;
And where there is sadness, joy.

ST. FRANCIS OF ASSISI

Peace is not the absence of affliction,
but the presence of God.

UNKNOWN

*The Son is the radiance of God's glory and the exact representation of his being, sustaining all things by his powerful word. After he had provided purification for sins, he sat down at the right hand of the Majesty in heaven.*

HEBREWS 1:3 NIV

*The one who loves his brother abides in the Light and there is no cause for stumbling in him.*

1 JOHN 2:10 NASB

God, there is so much darkness. I watch
the evening news and the stories are
of murder and loss and corruption.
Remind me of the greatest story of
all, the story of redemption, the story
of light. Thank You for my salvation,
purchased at Calvary with Your Son's
blood. Help me, Father, to light the
path for others that they might be led
to Him as well. Amen.

But if we live in the light, as God does,
we share in life with each other. And the blood
of his Son Jesus washes all our sins away.

1 JOHN 1:7 CEV

And do not be conformed to this world, but be
transformed by the renewing of your mind,
so that you may prove what the will of God is,
that which is good and acceptable and perfect.

ROMANS 12:2 NASB

Darkness cannot drive out darkness;
only light can do that. Hate cannot
drive out hate; only love can do that.

MARTIN LUTHER KING JR.

Through the clouds of midnight,
this bright promise shone, I will never
leave thee, never leave thee alone.

UNKNOWN

Holiness is doing God's
will with a smile.

MOTHER TERESA

Darkness cannot put out the light.
It can only make God brighter.

UNKNOWN

Remember this. When people choose to withdraw
far from a fire, the fire continues to give warmth,
but they grow cold. When people choose to
withdraw far from light, the light continues to be
bright in itself, but they are in darkness. This is
also the case when people withdraw from God.

AUGUSTINE

# The Songs
## of the
## Mountains

Seek the LORD while He may be found;
Call upon Him while He is near.
Let the wicked forsake his way
And the unrighteous man his thoughts;
And let him return to the LORD,
And He will have compassion on him,
And to our God,
For He will abundantly pardon. . . .
So will My word be which goes forth from My mouth;
It will not return to Me empty,
Without accomplishing what I desire,
And without succeeding in the
matter for which I sent it.
For you will go out with joy
And be led forth with peace;
The mountains and the hills will break
forth into shouts of joy before you,
And all the trees of the field will clap their hands."

ISAIAH 55:6–7; 11–12 NASB

❧

There is a condition here. The songs of the mountains and rejoicing of the trees are not without cause. The Lord is calling His people back to Himself in this chapter of Isaiah. Have you strayed from God? God's Word issues a distinct call back to Him.

God is so merciful! He stands ready to forgive. His grace is abundant, His love unending. But verse 6 says *"Seek the Lord while He may be found; call upon Him while He is near"* (NASB). The Bible tells of men who turned away from God so long that their hearts were hardened. They were no longer sensitive to the Lord's call.

If you have begun to walk with the world closer than you walk with the Lord, remember your heavenly Father today. If there a root of bitterness growing in your heart due to unforgiveness, lay it before your God. Ask Him to draw you close to Himself again. All creation will rejoice to see you return to your Father's embrace! Imagine it: He says the mountains will burst forth with song when His Word accomplishes this in your life. He says the trees will clap their hands!

"Instead of the thorn bush the cypress will come up,
And instead of the nettle the myrtle will come up,
And it will be a memorial to the LORD,
For an everlasting sign which will not be cut off."
ISAIAH 55:13 NASB

Burst into song, you mountains,
you forests and all your trees,
for the LORD has redeemed Jacob,
he displays his glory in Israel.
ISAIAH 44:23 NIV

Praise God, from whom
all blessings flow;
Praise Him, all creatures here below;
Praise Him above, ye heavenly host;
Praise Father, Son, and Holy Ghost.
Amen.

THE DOXOLOGY

THOMAS KEN

It's your kindness, Lord,
that leads us to repentance.
Your favor, Lord, is our desire.
It's your beauty, Lord,
that makes us stand in silence.
Your love, your love is better than life.

CHRIS TOMLIN

*Come, let us sing for joy to the L*ORD*;*
*let us shout aloud to the Rock of our salvation.*
PSALM 95:1 NIV

*I will bless the L*ORD *at all times; His praise shall*
*continually be in my mouth. My soul will make its*
*boast in the L*ORD*; the humble will hear it and rejoice.*
PSALM 34:1–3 NASB

Lord, may I honor you today in such a way that Your creation would rejoice! You are the maker of all things—the mountains, the valleys, all creatures large and small—and You are the creator and sustainer of my existence. If I start to follow the ways of the world, draw me back to Your side. There is no other way for me but the way of the Lord Almighty. Amen.

There is always music among the
trees in the garden, but our hearts
must be very quiet to hear it.

MINNIE AUMONIER

May flowers always line your path and sunshine
light your day. May songbirds serenade you every
step along the way. May a rainbow run beside you
in the sky that's always blue. And may happiness
fill your heart each day your whole life through.

IRISH BLESSING

Let the heavens rejoice,
and let the earth be glad;
And let them say among the nations,
"The LORD reigns."
Let the sea roar, and all its fullness;
Let the field rejoice, and all that is in it.
Then the trees of the woods shall
rejoice before the LORD,
For He is coming to judge the earth.
Oh, give thanks to the LORD, for He is good!
For His mercy endures forever.

1 CHRONICLES 16:31–34 NKJV

This is my Father's world,
And to my listening ears
All nature sings,
And round me rings
The music of the spheres.
This is my Father's world:
O let me ne'er forget
That though the wrong
Seems oft so strong,
God is the Ruler yet.

MALTBIE D. BABCOCK

God, in the stillness of an early morning I hear the birds sing their "good morning" to You! I listen in on their serenade before the King of kings, the created unable to contain its praise for the Creator. May You find me just as eager to bring my songs before You! I praise You, my King, through Jesus, my Savior, amen.

*Shout for joy, you heavens; rejoice, you earth; burst into song, you mountains! For the LORD comforts his people and will have compassion on his afflicted ones.*
ISAIAH 49:13 NIV

*Satisfy us in the morning with your unfailing love, that we may sing for joy and be glad all our days.*
PSALM 90:14 NIV

*Shout for joy to the LORD, all the earth, burst into jubilant song with music.*
PSALM 98:4 NIV

# Creation's
# Daily
# Inspiration

*For since the creation of the world God's invisible qualities—his eternal power and divine nature—have been clearly seen, being understood from what has been made, so that people are without excuse.*

ROMANS 1:20 NIV

❀

Creation tells of the Creator. It is that simple.

Watch waves crash in on the shore. Feel the strength of a storm, the warmth of a sun so bright you cannot look upon it. These are living products of the Master's hands. You have, in looking upon His creation, glimpsed His majesty. In the power of creation, find God's strength.

Examine an infant's tiny fingers. Breathe in deep the scents of lilacs and roses. Watch a baby deer begin to walk on wobbly legs. Taste the salt in your own tears as their release brings cleansing to your spirit. All of this did not just "come to be." It was designed, thought out.

organized, and crafted. . .by your Father.

Psalm 19 (NIV) says it like this:

*The heavens declare the glory of God;*
*the skies proclaim the work of his hands.*
*Day after day they pour forth speech;*
*night after night they reveal knowledge.*
*They have no speech, they use no words;*
*no sound is heard from them.*
*Yet their voice goes out into all the earth,*
*their words to the ends of the world.*

There is no denying the Creator. He has
given you creation. Find Him in it today.

*But the fruit of the Spirit is love, joy, peace,
longsuffering, kindness, goodness, faithfulness.*
GALATIANS 5:22 NKJV

*Everything in the Scriptures is God's Word. All of
it is useful for teaching and helping people and for
correcting them and showing them how to live.*
2 TIMOTHY 3:16 CEV

You will find something more in
woods than in books. Trees and
stones will teach you that which
you can never learn from masters.

St. Bernard

Lord, make us mindful of the little things
that grow and blossom in these days to
make the world beautiful for us.

W. E. B. DuBois

When I admire the wonder of a sunset
or the beauty of the moon, my soul
expands in worship of the Creator.

Crowfoot

Our LORD, let your worshipers
rejoice and be glad.
They love you for saving them,
so let them always say,
"The LORD is wonderful!"

PSALM 40:16 CEV

Lord, Your creation inspires me to love others better, to spend more time with my maker, and to please You with my time here upon this earth. May Your creation inspire me each day to live my life for You, my Creator. May I use the gifts and abilities You have given me to bring You glory. Amen.

Whenever I see sunbeams coming through the clouds, it always looks to me like God shining Himself down onto us. The thing about sunbeams is they're always there even though we can't see them. Same with God.

ADELINE CULLEN RAY

❀

Everyone must take time to sit
and watch the leaves turn.

ELIZABETH LAWRENCE

❀

Even if I knew that tomorrow
the world would go to pieces,
I would still plant my apple tree.

MARTIN LUTHER

This is the day which the LORD has made;
Let us rejoice and be glad in it.
PSALM 118:24 NASB

"Give us this day our daily bread."
MATTHEW 6:11 NASB

"Therefore do not worry about tomorrow,
for tomorrow will worry about itself.
Each day has enough trouble of its own."
MATTHEW 6:34 NIV

See how nature—trees, flowers, grass—grows in silence; see the stars, the moon, and the sun, how they move in silence. . . . We need silence to be able to touch souls.

MOTHER TERESA

Disturb us, Lord, to dare more boldly, to venture on wider seas where storms will show Your mastery.

SIR FRANCIS DRAKE

Weeds are flowers too, once you get to know them.

A. A. MILNE

Father, may I find the beauty in each day. When it rains, may I see that You are watering the earth, bringing forth flowers and green grass for us to enjoy. When the sun is hot, may I rejoice in its warmth rather than complaining. When the wind blows, let it be a reminder to me of Your power. May creation point me daily back to You, Lord. Amen.

If you've never been thrilled to the very
edges of your soul by a flower in spring bloom,
maybe your soul has never been in bloom.

AUDRA FOVEO

Beauty puts a face on God. When we
gaze at nature, at a loved one, at a work
of art, our soul immediately recognizes
and is drawn to the face of God.

MARGARET BROWNLEY

I've always regarded nature
as the clothing of God.

ALAN HOVHANESS

# Be Still and Know That He Is God

He says, "Be still, and know that I am God;
  I will be exalted among the nations,
  I will be exalted in the earth."
The LORD Almighty is with us;
  the God of Jacob is our fortress.

PSALM 46:10–11 NIV

❧

Mary was a busy woman. No one who knew her would deny that! She was a wife, a mother, and also held down a full-time job in the business world.

One day a frazzled coworker asked Mary how she did it all. "You never seem flustered. How do you do it?" The friend expected Mary to expose a special organization program or reveal that she had secretly hired a housekeeper and a cook! But it was nothing of the sort.

Mary smiled and said, "I don't do it all.

I learned a long time ago that I *can't* do it on my own. I have to rely on the Lord." Mary had discovered the secret of spending time with God. She took a few minutes each morning when the house was still quiet to go before her Creator God.

Often Mary came to her prayer time with burdens and concerns. Sometimes her heart was filled with joy and thanksgiving. Regardless of her circumstances, she always thanked God for simply *being* God. She sat quietly before Him, listening, acknowledging His sovereignty and His presence in her life.

Mary understood the meaning of being still and knowing that He is God.

"Abide in Me, and I in you. As the branch cannot bear fruit of itself, unless it abides in the vine, neither can you, unless you abide in Me. I am the vine, you are the branches. He who abides in Me, and I in him, bears much fruit; for without Me you can do nothing."

JOHN 15:4–5 NKJV

Now faith is the substance of things hoped for, the evidence of things not seen.

HEBREWS 11:1 NKJV

Adopt the pace of nature:
Her secret is patience.

RALPH WALDO EMERSON

The best remedy for those who are afraid,
lonely, or unhappy is to go outside,
somewhere where they can be quiet,
alone with the heavens, nature, and
God. Because only then does one feel
that all is as it should be.

ANNE FRANK

Climb up on some hill at sunrise.
Everybody needs perspective once
in a while, and you'll find it there.

ROBB SAGENDORPH

*Even though I walk through the darkest valley,*
*I will fear no evil, for you are with me;*
*your rod and your staff, they comfort me.*

PSALM 23:4 NIV

*For thus says the Lord GOD, the Holy One of Israel:*
*"In returning and rest you shall be saved;*
*In quietness and confidence shall be your strength."*

ISAIAH 30:15 NKJV

Lord, I am constantly pulled at to be *busy*, not *still*! There are so many demands on my every day, my every moment. But You ask me to be still. You are the one in my life who truly wants me all to Yourself. You tell me to be still and know that You are God. I know the rest will fall into place. Teach me to be still, I pray. Amen.

*He who dwells in the shelter of the Most High*
*will abide in the shadow of the Almighty.*

PSALM 91:1 NASB

*"I have come as a light into the world, that whoever*
*believes in Me should not abide in darkness."*

JOHN 12:46 NKJV

*He makes me to lie down in green pastures;*
*He leads me beside the still waters. He restores my soul.*

PSALM 23:2–3 NKJV

I love to think of nature as an
unlimited broadcasting station,
through which God speaks to us
every hour, if we only tune in.

GEORGE WASHINGTON CARVER

When you take a flower in your
hand and really look at it,
it's your world for the moment.

GEORGIA O'KEEFE

The human spirit needs places
where nature has not been
rearranged by the hand of man.

UNKNOWN

"Cease striving and know that I am God."
PSALM 46:10 NASB

❈

Cast all your anxiety on him because he cares for you.
1 PETER 5:7 NIV

❈

He calms the storm,
So that its waves are still.
PSALM 107:29 NKJV

❈

A dry crust of bread eaten
in peace and quiet
is better than a feast eaten
where everyone argues.
PROVERBS 17:1 CEV

Help me, Father, to find a place to rest before You. I know that You can meet me on my patio or by the lake at the park. The country road canopied by trees is just as desirable to You as the spot on the deserted beach. Help me not to neglect quiet time with You in Your creation. Show me a place where we can meet, just Father and daughter. I love You, Lord.

Rest is not idleness, and to lie sometimes
on the grass on a summer day listening to the
murmur of water, or watching the clouds float
across the sky, is hardly a waste of time.

JOHN LUBBOCK

Only God can fully satisfy
the hungry heart of man.

HUGH BLACK

# He's Not
# Finished Yet

I thank my God every time I remember you. In all my prayers for all of you, I always pray with joy because of your partnership in the gospel from the first day until now, being confident of this, that he who began a good work in you will carry it on to completion until the day of Christ Jesus.

PHILIPPIANS 1:3–6 NIV

❀

Do you feel that God is disappointed in you? Have you fallen into a bad habit or gone down a wrong path? Maybe it is a divorce or another damaged relationship in your life that causes you to believe God has given up on you.

Nothing could be further from the truth. God loves you just as much today as He did when you were an innocent infant. He's not finished with you yet. Throughout your life, God will use circumstances and even disappointments to perfect you. Our heavenly Father never gives up on His children.

Paul reminds the Philippians that God has begun a good work in them and that He will be faithful to complete it. When does Paul say that completion will be? He clearly states that it will not be until *the day of Christ Jesus*.

Mankind is God's most prized creation. Even the angels are a little lower than mankind! Ask the Lord to help you as you seek to walk in His ways. He will be faithful. There will be times when you have regrets or need to choose to get back on the right road. But remember: God's not finished with you yet!

*Wait for the LORD; be strong and let your*
*heart take courage; yes, wait for the LORD.*
PSALM 27:14 NASB

*For I am convinced that neither death, nor life, nor*
*angels, nor principalities, nor things present, nor things*
*to come, nor powers, nor height, nor depth, nor any*
*other created thing, will be able to separate us from*
*the love of God, which is in Christ Jesus our Lord.*
ROMANS 8:38–39 NASB

God is the perfect poet.
ROBERT BROWNING

❖

Gold cannot be pure,
and people cannot be perfect.
CHINESE PROVERB

❖

In nature we see where God has
been. In our fellow man, we see
where He is still at work.
ROBERT BRAULT

❖

I believe in the sun even if it isn't
shining. I believe in love even when
I am alone. I believe in God even
when He is silent.
UNKNOWN

*Truly my soul finds rest in God; my salvation
comes from him. . . . Yes, my soul, find rest
in God; my hope comes from him.*

PSALM 62:1, 5 NIV

*And we know that God causes all things to
work together for good to those who love God,
to those who are called according to His purpose.*

ROMANS 8:28 NASB

Lord, I get impatient with myself. At the end of another busy day, I often reflect on my shortcomings. How could I have lost my temper that way? Why wasn't I more patient? Thank You for the reminder that You aren't finished with me yet. I am a work in progress. Make me moldable, Father, like clay in a potter's hands. Change me. Make me a little more like Jesus every day, I ask. Amen.

This is life we've been given, made
to be lived out, so. . .live out loud.
STEVEN CURTIS CHAPMAN

❀

The imperfections of a man, his frailties,
his faults, are just as important as his virtues.
You can't separate them. They're wedded.
HENRY MILLER

❀

What we are is God's gift to us.
What we become is our gift to God.
ELEANOR POWELL

"My sheep hear My voice, and I know them,
and they follow Me. And I give them eternal
life, and they shall never perish; neither shall
anyone snatch them out of My hand.
My Father, who has given them to Me,
is greater than all; and no one is able to
snatch them out of My Father's hand."

JOHN 10:27–29 NKJV

" 'He will wipe every tear from their eyes.
There will be no more death' or mourning or crying or
pain, for the old order of things has passed away."
REVELATION 21:4 NIV

Praise the LORD. . .who satisfies your desires with good
things so that your youth is renewed like the eagle's.
PSALM 103:2, 5 NIV

Heavenly Father, I look at Your creation in amazement. To think that You created the earth in only six days is beyond my comprehension. And You are still creating new life every day! A baby's birth and an old man's profession of faith in Christ. . .both are symbols that my God is still in the business of creating! Thank You, Lord, for new life and for second chances. Amen.

It's always too early to quit.

NORMAN VINCENT PEALE

❖

When you pray for anyone you tend to
modify your personal attitude toward him.

NORMAN VINCENT PEALE

❖

Promise me you'll always remember: you're
braver than you believe, and stronger than
you seem, and smarter than you think.

A. A. MILNE

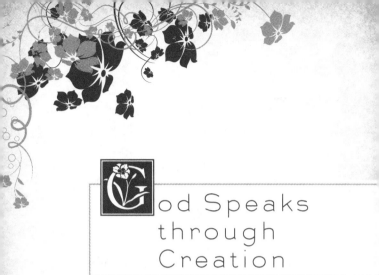

# God Speaks through Creation

*How many are your works, LORD!*
*In wisdom you made them all;*
*the earth is full of your creatures.*
PSALM 104:24 NIV

❁

The chirping of birds in springtime, the whisper of the wind as it blows through your hair on an early morning jog. . . . Have you considered these to be the very voice of the Creator? God speaks through His creation. Sometimes it may be the deep rumble of thunder followed by a flash of lightning, and other times the whimper of a warm puppy so small that you can hold him in one hand.

As you go throughout your day today, take notice of the world around you. Where do you see God? Where do you hear your Creator's voice? God reveals Himself to His children in personal ways. He desires an intimate, one on one relationship with each son and daughter. You may meet God on snowcapped mountains while skiing at amazing speed or you may find Him as you rest beside a quiet pond at the neighborhood park.

The important thing is that you listen. Don't miss God in His creation. He wants to speak to you. He wants to show Himself real to you. He is the maker of all things and He is reflected through His creation—if only we take time to notice.

"Never again will the waters become a flood to destroy all life. Whenever the rainbow appears in the clouds, I will see it and remember the everlasting covenant between God and all living creatures of every kind on the earth." So God said to Noah, "This is the sign of the covenant I have established between me and all life on the earth."

GENESIS 9:15–17 NIV

If the sight of the blue skies fills you with joy, if a blade of grass springing up in the field has power to move you, if the simple things of nature have a message that you understand, rejoice, for your soul is alive.

ELEONORA DUSE

❦

I think that if ever a mortal heard the voice of God it would be in a garden at the cool of the day.

F. FRANKFORT MOORE

*Whether you turn to the right or to the left,*
*you will hear a voice saying,*
*"This is the road! Now follow it."*
Isaiah 30:21 cev

Father, sometimes I look for writing in the sky or listen for a booming voice from heaven. I search earnestly to know Your will and Your direction for my life. I love the times when I remember to rest quietly before You in Your creation. Nature has a way of calming my spirit and drawing me into Your presence. Speak to me through creation, God. Comfort my weary mind and give me direction, I pray. Amen.

The best place to seek God is in a garden.

GEORGE BERNARD SHAW

❀

If people sat outside and looked at the stars
each night, I'll bet they'd live a lot differently.

BILL WATTERSON

❀

I can enjoy society in a room; but out of doors,
nature is company enough for me.

WILLIAM HAZLITT

"The gatekeeper opens the gate for him,
and the sheep listen to his voice. He calls
his own sheep by name and leads them out.
When he has brought out all his own, he goes
on ahead of them, and his sheep follow him
because they know his voice."

JOHN 10:3-4 NIV

I will listen to you, LORD God,
because you promise peace to those
who are faithful and no longer foolish.

PSALM 85:8 CEV

Preach the gospel always,
and when absolutely necessary, use words.

ST. FRANCIS OF ASSISI

❧

Morning has broken
Like the first morning,
Blackbird has spoken
Like the first bird.
Praise for the singing!
Praise for the morning!
Praise for them, springing
Fresh from the Word!

FROM "MORNING HAS BROKEN"
ELEANOR FARJEON

❧

If God had wanted to be a big secret,
He would not have created babbling
brooks and whispering pines.

ROBERT BRAULT

I think I have discovered, Lord,
Your still small voice. I hear it in
the trickling of the brook and in
the songs of birds. I have heard
Your power, Father, in storms and
crashing waves. You are ever present
in Your creation. When I have spent
time in Your creation, I have spent
time with the Creator. Amen.

*You are my dove*
*hiding among the rocks*
*on the side of a cliff.*
*Let me see how lovely you are!*
*Let me hear the sound*
*of your melodious voice.*

SONG OF SOLOMON 2:14 CEV

# The Lord
# God Made
# Them All

*od saw all that he had made, and it*
*was very good. And there was evening,*
*and there was morning—the sixth day.*

GENESIS 1:31 NIV

❀

There is a popular children's book that tells
the story of a cricket who does not want to be a
cricket. He admires the appearance and abilities
of other animals and wishes that he could be
more like them. Are we so different from the
cricket?

It is a strong tendency of most women to
compare ourselves with others. We wish we
could be thinner or more organized, have curly
hair instead of straight—or straight instead of
curly!

When was the last time you considered
that the Lord God made you? He made you

*just the way you are.* He knit you together in your mother's womb, weaving together in the secret place a perfect combination of traits and talents.

God made the world and everything in it. Genesis tells us that He then sat back and smiled. Well, not in so many words! But it says He saw His creation and was *pleased.*

God is delighted with the details that make you who you are. Instead of wishing you were someone else, examine your abilities. You are not called to be what you are not, but you are called to make the most of what you are.

Use the talents you possess—for the woods
would be a very silent place if no birds
sang except for the very best.

HENRY VAN DYKE

❧

There is a God-shaped vacuum in every heart.

BLAISE PASCAL

❧

The gateway to Christianity is not through
an intricate labyrinth of dogma, but by
a simple belief in the person of Christ.

NORMAN VINCENT PEALE

Every creature, every plant, every star in the heavens above. . . They are all from Your hands. God, it is easy to thank You for the sweet-smelling rose or warm summer sunshine. I don't feel so thankful for the person in my life who hurts me with rude comments! Give me patience, Lord, as I seek to treat others around me as other children of the Creator. In Jesus' name I pray, amen.

*Everything God created is good. And if you give thanks,
you may eat anything. What God has said and your
prayer will make it fit to eat.*

1 TIMOTHY 4:4-5 CEV

*"Six days you shall labor and do all your work,
but the seventh day is a sabbath to the LORD your God.
On it you shall not do any work, neither you,
nor your son or daughter."*

EXODUS 20:9-10 NIV

Holy, holy, holy!
Lord God Almighty!
All Thy works shall praise
Thy name in earth and sky and sea;
Holy, holy, holy!
Merciful and mighty!
God in three persons,
Blessed Trinity!

FROM "HOLY, HOLY, HOLY,
LORD GOD ALMIGHTY"

REGINALD HEBER

It is of practical value to learn to
like yourself. Since you must spend
so much time with yourself you might
as well get some satisfaction out
of the relationship.

NORMAN VINCENT PEALE

The man said, "This is now bone of my bones,
And flesh of my flesh;
She shall be called Woman,
Because she was taken out of Man."

Genesis 2:23 nasb

Heavenly Father, You are the Alpha and the Omega, the beginning and the end. You are before all things and above all things. May I never worship the creation, but may it continue to point me to the Creator all the days of my life. Thank You for the blessing of a beautiful world in which to live and for the promise of eternity with You. Amen.

*Praise the* L*ord*, *my soul*;
*all my inmost being*, *praise his holy name*.

PSALM 103:1 NIV